CRIME Solvers

Kidnapping FILE
The Graeme Thorne Case

by Amanda Howard

Consultant: Dr. John P. Cassella
Principal Lecturer in Forensic Science
Staffordshire University, England

BEARPORT
PUBLISHING

New York, New York

Credits

Cover, © Mary Lane/istockphoto and © Newspix/News Ltd/3rd Party Managed Reproduction & Supply Rights; Title Page, © Newspix/News Ltd/3rd Party Managed Reproduction & Supply Rights; 4, © Shutterstock; 5, © Newspix / News Ltd.; 6T, © Newspix/News Ltd/3rd Party Managed Reproduction & Supply Rights; 6C, © ticktock Media Archive; 6B, © Shutterstock; 7, © Courtesy of the Australian Police Journal–July 1962 issue; 8, © Newspix/News Ltd/3rd Party Managed Reproduction & Supply Rights; 9, © Fairfax photos; 10, © Newspix/News Ltd/3rd Party Managed Reproduction & Supply Rights; 11T, © Shutterstock; 11B, © Shutterstock; 12, © Fairfax photos; 13T, © SeriousWheels.com; 13B, © Shutterstock; 14, © Fairfax photos; 15, © Courtesy of the Australian Police Journal–July 1962 issue; 16, © Newspix/News Ltd/3rd Party Managed Reproduction & Supply Rights; 17T, © Courtesy of the Australian Police Journal–July 1962 issue; 17B, © Science Photo Library/David Scharf; 18T, © iStock International Inc/Rebecca Dickerson; 18B, © Shutterstock; 19T, © Newspix/News Ltd/3rd Party Managed Reproduction & Supply Rights; 19B, © Shutterstock; 20, © Newspix/News Ltd/3rd Party Managed Reproduction & Supply Rights; 21, © Shutterstock; 22, © Science Photo Library/John McLean; 23T, © Science Photo Library/Zephyr; 23B, © Michael D. Hunter M.D; 24, © Newspix/News Ltd/3rd Party Managed Reproduction & Supply Rights; 25T, © A Y Arktos; 25B, © Brand X Pictures/fotosearch.com; 28, © Science Photo Library/Tek Image; 29, © Rex Features; 30, © Shutterstock.

Every effort has been made by ticktock Entertainment Ltd. to trace copyright holders. We apologize in advance for any omissions. We would be pleased to insert the appropriate acknowledgments in any subsequent edition of this publication.

Publisher: Kenn Goin
Editorial Director: Adam Siegel
Project Editor: Dinah Dunn
Creative Director: Spencer Brinker
Original Design: ticktock Entertainment Ltd.

Library of Congress Cataloging-in-Publication Data

Howard, Amanda, 1973–
   Kidnapping file : the Graeme Thorne case / by Amanda Howard.
      p. cm. — (Crime solvers)
   Includes bibliographical references and index.
   ISBN-13: 978-1-59716-548-8 (library binding)
   ISBN-10: 1-59716-548-4 (library binding)
   1. Thorne, Graeme. 2. Kidnapping—Australia—Case studies—Juvenile literature. I. Title.

   HV6604.A82T55 2008
   364.15'4092—dc22

                              2007016519

10 9 8 7 6 5 4 3 2 1

Contents

Good Luck Turns Bad

Eight-year-old Graeme Thorne and his family were thrilled. On June 1, 1960, they won Sydney's Opera House **lottery**. The first prize was £100,000, which today would be worth around $4 million. Newspapers all over Australia ran front-page stories about their incredible luck.

The money didn't really change the Thorne family's life. They still lived in an apartment in Bondi, a beachside suburb of Sydney, Australia. Graeme's father, Bazil, continued working as a traveling salesman. Each morning Graeme still walked to the corner where neighbor Phyllis Smith picked him up for school. However, their life wasn't going to stay the same for long.

On July 7, 1960, Graeme put on his school uniform and packed his lunch in his book bag. He called good-bye to his little sister and walked out the door. He was never seen alive again.

Bondi Beach, where Graeme liked to go swimming

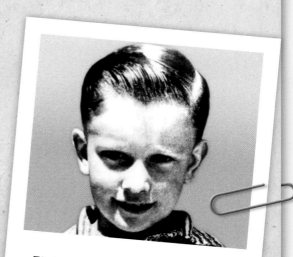

Eight-year-old Graeme Thorne

A Dangerous Plan

Stephen Bradley had read about the Thornes' lottery win in the newspaper. How could he get his hands on that money? He soon came up with a plan.

Bradley called the lottery office. He got the Thornes' address and telephone number from them. Next, he went to the Thornes' house.

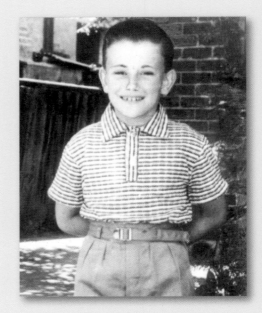

Graeme Thorne in happier times

The winning lottery ticket

The lottery helped raise money to build the Sydney Opera House.

Graeme's mother, Freda, answered the door. She was greeted by a man wearing dark glasses. In a heavy **accent**, Bradley asked her if Mr. Bognor was home. Mrs. Thorne said nobody with that name lived there. He then asked if the phone number he had for her house was correct. She said it was and the strange man left.

Ordinarily, Mrs. Thorne would have forgotten the meeting. She had spoken with the man for only a few minutes. However, the next time she heard his voice, he would have horrifying news.

FACT FILE

Who Was Stephen Bradley?

- Stephen Bradley was born Istvan Baranyay in 1926 in Budapest, Hungary.

- He moved to Australia in 1950.

- He changed his name to Stephen Leslie Bradley.

- His first wife died in a car accident.

- He had remarried and had three children at the time of the crime.

Stephen Bradley

The Kidnapping

Stephen Bradley secretly watched the Thorne family for weeks. He noticed that Graeme was picked up for school every day at 8:30 A.M.

On July 7, 1960, Bradley drove to the corner of O'Brien and Wellington streets. He was ready to carry out his plan.

That morning, Graeme was not waiting at the corner when Mrs. Smith came to pick him up. Graeme's mother was worried, but thought he might have gotten a ride from someone else. When he didn't arrive at school, Mrs. Thorne became frightened. She called the police.

The corner where Graeme disappeared

Within minutes, Sergeant Larry O'Shea was at the door. He was taking notes when the phone rang. Mrs. Thorne answered. A man with a heavy accent asked to speak with her husband. "What do you want my husband for?" she asked.

"I have your son, Mrs. Thorne," the man replied.

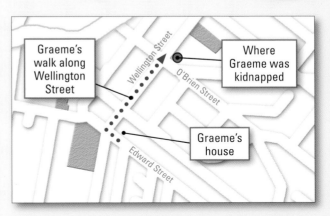

This map shows Graeme's path to the corner where he was kidnapped.

A young witness shows police where she last saw Graeme.

FACT FILE

Where Did Bradley Get the Idea?

- In April 1960, four-year-old Eric Peugeot, the son of a Paris automobile millionaire, was taken from a playground. His **kidnappers** demanded $100,000 for the boy's safe return. When the **ransom** was paid, Eric was returned unharmed. His kidnappers were arrested two years later.

- When Bradley kidnapped Graeme, Peugeot's kidnappers had not yet been caught. Some people believe this kidnapping gave Bradley the idea for his crime.

The Ransom

Graeme's father was not home when Bradley called, so Mrs. Thorne gave the phone to Sergeant O'Shea. He pretended to be Mr. Thorne and asked what the man wanted.

Bradley asked for £25,000, which would be worth $1 million in today's money. He wanted the ransom before 5:00 that afternoon. "If you don't get the money I'll feed the boy to the sharks." Bradley said he would call back later and hung up.

Sharks are often spotted near the beaches in Australia.

The police called an immediate **press conference**. That afternoon, newspapers carried the shocking story of Australia's first kidnapping. Police quickly began a huge search operation to find the boy.

Graeme Thorne's parents at a press conference

At 9:47 P.M. that evening, Stephen Bradley phoned again. He gave instructions to put the money into two paper bags, and then hung up. When he didn't call back, Graeme's father went on television. He begged the kidnapper to "send [Graeme] back to me in one piece."

FACT FILE

Freda Thorne Recognizes Bradley's Voice

- After Bradley called, Mrs. Thorne remembered hearing his voice before.

- She told police of his earlier visit and the man became the **prime suspect**.

- Police drove her around the area near the kidnapping to see if she could spot him.

A Clue Is Discovered

The next day, on July 8, 1960, a man found Graeme's empty book bag a few miles away from Bondi. He immediately called the police, who swarmed the area. Within days, searchers found Graeme's coat, lunch bag, and math book. There was no sign of the boy, however. Was he still alive?

Hundreds of police searched near the area where Graeme's book bag was found.

Police also followed up on a **lead** they had received. A young man had spotted a blue 1955 Ford Customline at the scene of the kidnapping. Police began interviewing thousands of people in the area who owned this type of car. They also asked people to report anyone with a 1955 Ford who had been acting **suspiciously**.

A 1955 Ford Customline car was spotted double-parked at the crime scene.

FACT FILE
Graeme's Book Bag

- Graeme's book bag was dusted for **fingerprints**.

- The police used a colored powder that makes fingerprints visible.

- The fingerprints did not match any known criminals.

- After Bradley's arrest, police discovered that his fingerprints matched those on the book bag.

Graeme carried a book bag like this one to school.

From Kidnapping to Murder

A month later, two boys discovered a bundle while playing in an empty lot in Seaforth, a town several miles from Graeme's house. They didn't know about the kidnapping, so they didn't tell anyone about their discovery right away. Then a few weeks later they mentioned the bundle to a friend. He told his parents and the police were soon called.

On August 16, almost six weeks after he was kidnapped, Graeme's dead body was found. He was wrapped in a blanket. His hands and feet were tied with a rope. A silk scarf was tied around his neck.

The police thought Graeme had died from either **suffocation** or a head injury or from both. They searched the area for **clues** using helicopters and dogs. The kidnapping case had now become a murder hunt.

Police dogs were used to search for clues.

When the news about Graeme's body appeared in the paper, the police received a call. A couple living in a town next to Seaforth told police about their neighbor. He had a blue 1955 Ford Customline and had moved out of his house the day of Graeme's kidnapping. His name was Stephen Bradley.

FACT FILE

Australians are Shocked

- Australians never thought anyone in their country would be kidnapped.

- When Graeme was kidnapped, there wasn't even a law against it.

- In 2004, 768 people in Australia were kidnapped.

Graeme's body was found in this empty lot.

The Crime Scene

The area where Graeme was found became a **crime scene**. His body and the blanket were carefully examined for clues. **Forensic** experts found **traces** of two types of cypress trees that did not grow in the lot. They also found human and animal hair, as well as some pink sand. The animal hair was determined to be from a Pekingese dog. The sand was **mortar** from a pink house.

Detectives searched for clues in the blanket that had been wrapped around Graeme's body.

Police also followed up on the tip from Stephen Bradley's neighbors. They interviewed Bradley at his job.

Bradely had an **alibi** for the morning Graeme was kidnapped. He said he was moving out of his house to an apartment nearby. Police checked with the moving company. They confirmed his story. Bradley was off the hook! He immediately sold his belongings and bought tickets for his family on a ship sailing to England.

The blanket in which Graeme was wrapped

FACT FILE

When Did Graeme Die?

Forensic experts **estimated** that Graeme died within 24 hours of his kidnapping based on this evidence:

- **Fungi** had grown on Graeme's shoes. It had taken three weeks to grow and three weeks to reproduce.

- From this **evidence** they could tell that Graeme had died on July 7, 1960, six weeks before his body was discovered. Graeme had probably been killed the same day he disappeared.

Fungi under a microscope

Closing In on a Suspect

Although they had a number of clues, investigators were no closer to finding out who had kidnapped Graeme. Then the movers called back. They had been mistaken. They hadn't moved Bradley in the morning, but in the afternoon.

Bradley now no longer had an alibi. Police began to build a case against him. They went to the house in Clontarf that Bradley had moved out of on the day of the kidnapping. Jackpot! It had both pink mortar and cypress trees.

Police still hadn't found the dog whose hair was discovered with Graeme's body. A person who lived in Clontarf, however, told police he had seen a **veterinarian**'s van in Bradley's driveway.

Police called the vet and found Cherry, Bradley's Pekingese dog. She was being held there until she could be shipped to England. Her hair matched the ones found by investigators.

Pink mortar was used between the bricks of Bradley's house.

Cypress trees like these grew near Bradley's house.

Police asked the media for help finding Bradley's blue Ford. A car dealer called to say he had bought the car from Bradley. Police recovered it and vacuumed out the trunk. Investigators found hair, plants, and sand similar to those found on Graeme's body. It appeared that Graeme had been kept a prisoner in the trunk. Police now had all of the evidence they needed to arrest Bradley.

Stephen Bradley's house in Clontarf

A Pekingese dog like Bradley's

FACT FILE
The Blanket

- Police found film negatives near Bradley's home.

- When the photos were developed, they showed Bradley's family sitting on a blanket.

- The blanket looked exactly the same as the one police had found wrapped around Graeme's body!

The Arrest

Police could not arrest Stephen Bradley right away. He was with his family on a ship heading to England. They learned that the ship's journey included a stop in Colombo, Ceylon (now called Sri Lanka). When the Bradley family arrived there on October 10, 1960, the police were waiting for them.

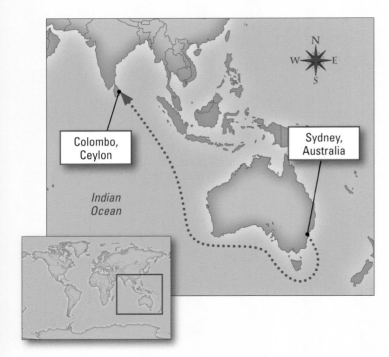

The Bradleys' route from Sydney to Colombo

Stephen Bradley (left) was arrested as he left the ship at Colombo.

Stephen Bradley was arrested and flown back to Sydney. On the flight, he said he had kidnapped Graeme and put him in his car trunk. Yet he claimed that Graeme had died accidentally.

Once back in Sydney, Bradley said the police had forced him to confess to a crime he didn't commit. Police, however, had enough evidence to prove he had kidnapped Graeme. What they didn't know was whether Graeme's death was an accident or a murder.

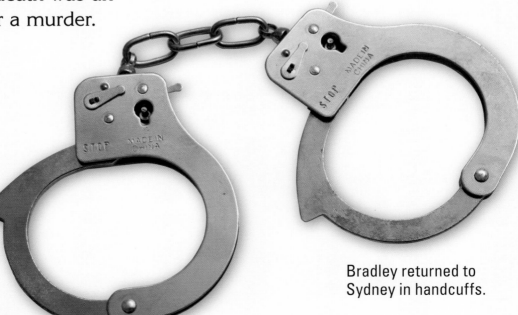

Bradley returned to Sydney in handcuffs.

The Autopsy

Bradley's lawyers said that Graeme's death was an accident. **Forensic pathologists** performed an autopsy on the boy's body to determine the cause of death. They found that a blow to the back of his head could have killed Graeme. Tests showed that the wound was too deep to be caused by Graeme accidentally bumping his head in the trunk. Someone had hit him.

A modern pathologist preparing for an autopsy

Bradley's lawyers also suggested that Graeme could have died from suffocating in the trunk of the car. Scientists tested the air in the trunk over several hours. There was enough oxygen to keep a person alive. In addition, Graeme had small red spots on his lungs and throat, which is a sign of being strangled.

Pathologists determined that Graeme's death was not an accident. He had been murdered.

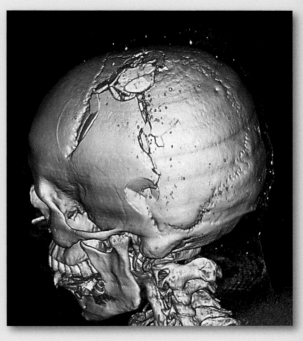

A violent blow cracked this skull. Graeme Thorne was injured in a similar way.

FACT FILE

What Is an Autopsy?

- An autopsy is an examination of a dead body by specially trained doctors called pathologists.

- The purpose of an autopsy is to answer questions about what caused a person's death.

- An autopsy usually takes two to four hours to perform.

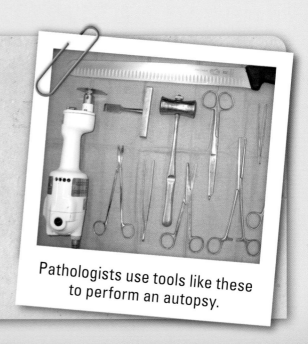

Pathologists use tools like these to perform an autopsy.

The Trial

Stephen Bradley's murder trial began on March 19, 1961. The courtroom was so packed that hundreds of people were turned away. Everyone wanted to see the monster who had killed an eight-year-old boy.

The judge stated that the **jury** must consider all the evidence in the case. They must be sure beyond a shadow of a doubt that Bradley had kidnapped and murdered Graeme Thorne.

Graeme's father, Bazil Thorne, arriving at the trial

Ten days later, the jury found Bradley guilty. The courtroom erupted in cheers and applause. Many people shouted that Stephen Bradley should be fed to the sharks, as he had threatened to do to Graeme. The judge told Stephen Bradley he had to spend the rest of his life in prison.

Goulburn Gaol, the prison where Bradley was sent

FACT FILE

What Happened to Stephen Bradley?

- In June 1961, Bradley started serving his life sentence at Goulburn Gaol, a prison in New South Wales, Australia.

- He died of a heart attack on October 6, 1968. Bradley was 42 years old.

Bradley spent the last seven years of his life in prison.

Case Closed

June 1, 1960

Bazil Thorne wins £100,000 in the Sydney Opera House Lottery.

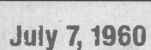

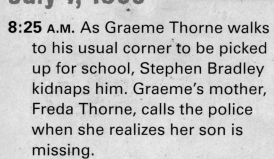

July 7, 1960

8:25 A.M. As Graeme Thorne walks to his usual corner to be picked up for school, Stephen Bradley kidnaps him. Graeme's mother, Freda Thorne, calls the police when she realizes her son is missing.

9:20 A.M. Bradley calls the Thorne home. He says that he wants £25,000 or he will "feed the boy to the sharks."

9:47 P.M. Bradley calls again to see if the money is ready for him. Mrs. Thorne recognizes Bradley's voice from the visit he made to their home a few weeks earlier.

July 8, 1960

- Graeme's book bag is found.

August 16, 1960

- Graeme's body is found wrapped in a blanket. Traces of pink mortar, dog hairs, and two different kinds of cypress trees are found at the crime

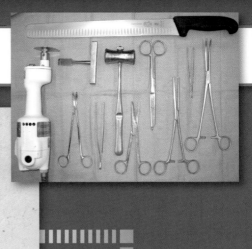

August 17, 1960

- An autopsy shows that Graeme died within 24 hours of his kidnapping. He died from either a blow to the head or from being strangled.

October 1960

- Police officers go to Stephen Bradley's house. Trees near the house are the same kind as those found on the blanket. The house has pink mortar between the bricks. Police find Bradley's dog, Cherry, at a local vet.

- Stephen Bradley is arrested in Colombo on October 10.

March 19, 1961

The trial of Stephen Bradley begins.

March 29, 1961

Stephen Bradley is found guilty of the kidnapping and murder of Graeme Thorne. He is sentenced to life in prison.

October 6, 1968

Stephen Bradley dies in

Crime Solving Up Close

Trace Evidence Retrieval

In the Graeme Thorne case, the blanket the boy's body was wrapped in provided police with a mountain of evidence against his killer. Yet all of this evidence could probably fit in the palm of one's hand. How do police find such tiny clues?

- A piece of evidence, such as a blanket or an item of clothing, is taken from the crime scene to a laboratory.

- Photographs are taken of the evidence.

- Scientists begin a careful search of the item.

- They look for tiny clues, such as hair, dirt, fibers, or plants. This trace evidence is carefully collected and placed into a bag.

- Hair, fibers, dirt, or other items connected to the suspect are compared to the collected evidence. A match can provide proof that a suspect was at a crime scene.

An investigator uses tweezers to lift a hair from a cracked window.

Estimating the Time of Death

Pathologists studied the growth of fungi on Graeme's shoes to figure out how long he had been dead. Here are some other ways pathologists estimate the time of a person's death.

- **Rigor mortis:** After death, a person's muscles tighten and stiffen. By measuring how stiff the body has become, pathologists can tell how long someone has been dead.

- **Decomposition:** The longer a dead body is left untouched, the more it decays. It takes several years for the flesh to completely disappear. Experts look at patterns of decay to estimate the time and date of death.

- **Food digestion:** When someone dies, his or her body stops digesting food. Pathologists can check the contents of the stomach against the person's last known meal to predict the time of death.

- **Entomology:** The study of insects is called entomology. Forensic pathologists look at how long insects have been growing in a dead body and whether they have reproduced. This growth pattern helps them determine how long a body has been dead.

A forensic pathologist looks at the growth of insects in a body.

Crime Solving Up Close

Fingerprint Matching

The examination of fingerprints has been used in court cases for more than 100 years. The police found fingerprints on Graeme's book bag that later matched Stephen Bradley's. How can fingerprints help solve a crime?

- Fingerprints are unique. No two people have the same fingerprint.

- Fingerprints do not change over the course of a person's life.

There are eight main types of fingerprint patterns:

plain arch   tented arch   plain whorl   accidental

radial loop (if on left hand)   central pocket loop   double-loop whorl   ulnar loop (if on left hand)

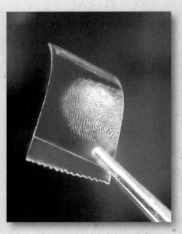

Fingerprints can be lifted from surfaces with sticky tape.

- Any person convicted of a crime has his or her fingerprints recorded by an electric scanner. These are kept in a database so that they can be checked against unsolved and future crimes.

Glossary

accent (AK-sent) a way of pronouncing words

alibi (AL-i-*bye*) a claim by a person accused of a crime that he or she was somewhere else when the crime was committed

clues (KLOOZ) objects or information used to solve a mystery

crime scene (KRIME SEEN) an area where an illegal act has taken place

estimated (ESS-ti-*mate*-id) figured out the approximate amount

evidence (EV-uh-duhnss) objects or information that can be used to prove whether something is true

fingerprints (FING-gur-prints) the impressions made by the pattern of curved ridges on the tips of one's fingers

forensic (fuh-REN-sik) using science and technology to help solve crimes

forensic pathologists (fuh-REN-sik path-OL-uh-*jists*) doctors who study dead bodies to find out the cause of death

fungi (FUHN-jye) plant-like organisms that have no flowers or leaves

jury (JU-ree) a group of people that listen to facts at a trial and make a decision about who is to blame

kidnappers (KID-nap-urz) people who capture and keep another person until certain demands are met

lead (LEED) a piece of useful advice or information

lineup (LINE-uhp) the arrangement of a number of people in a row where a witness to a crime is asked to identify the person who committed the crime

lottery (LOT-ur-ee) a way of raising money in which people buy tickets in order to try to win a prize

mortar (MOR-tur) a mixture of sand, lime, water, and cement that is spread and hardened between bricks or stones to hold them together

press conference (PRESS KON-fur-uhnss) a meeting where people can share important information with reporters

prime suspect (PRIME SUHSS-pekt) a person who is thought most likely to have committed a crime

ransom (RAN-suhm) money that is demanded for the release of a person being held captive

suffocation (*suhf*-uh-KAY-shun) being killed by having one's supply of air stopped

suspiciously (suh-SPISH-uhss-lee) a way of acting that causes question or doubt

traces (TRAYSS-iz) small amounts

veterinarian (*vet*-ur-uh-NER-ee-uhn) a doctor who treats animals

Index

Read More

Hunter, William. *Mark and Trace Analysis.* Philadelphia, PA: Mason Crest Publishers (2006).

Lane, Brian, and Laura Buller. *Crime & Detection.* New York: Dorling Kindersley (2005).

Owen, David. *Police Lab: How Forensic Science Tracks Down and Convicts Criminals.* Canada: Firefly Books (2002).

Learn More Online

To learn more about crime solving and the Graeme Thorne case, visit **www.bearportpublishing.com/CrimeSolvers**

About the Author

Amanda Howard writes extensively about true crime, including the encyclopedia *River of Blood: Serial Killers and Their Victims.* She is currently studying for her Bachelor of Social Science in Criminology, Criminal Law, and Psychology. She lives near Sydney, Australia, with her family.